HMO PREPAID METERS

Everything You Want and Need To Know About Fitting Prepaid Meters in HMOs

C.J. Haliburton

BA DMS Cert Ed

Experienced landlord with over
100 HMOs and 1000 tenants.

www.hmodaddy.com

C.J. Haliburton
14 Walsall Road
Wednesbury
WS10 9Jl

Print Edition

ISBN: 978-1-4467-0385-4

Contents

WARNING

Jim Haliburton, known as HMO Daddy, is not an electrician, energy conservation expert, lawyer or financial advisor, nor does the following represent legal, financial or any other advice. If such advice is needed, then the reader should seek professional guidance from a qualified expert with appropriate public liability insurance. The following information is given to the best of Jim Haliburton's knowledge and is provided for educational purposes only. It is the reader's responsibility to obtain their own professional advice.

ACKNOWLEDGEMENT

I would like to thank all the HMO landlords and the people who are thinking about getting into the industry for their questions, because this has made writing this book easy for me. All I had to do was ask my assistant Toni Neal to collate the questions on meters and present them in this book. Any errors are entirely down to me.

FREE UPDATE

As this is the first edition of the book, there will no doubt be some mistakes. These are all down to me, the author.

If you would like the next corrected and maybe updated/revised edition, then complete your details below along with your receipt, and I will send you a downloadable copy of the next edition FREE OF CHARGE with no obligation.

If you have anything you wish to contribute, questions or comments to make, please add below or send us a separate email to jim@hmodaddy.com

_____

_____

_____

_____

Name: _____

Email address: _____

How did you purchase your original copy of the book? _____

Your details will be added to my database. If you do NOT wish for them to be entered, please put a cross in the box ☐

EMAIL WITH A COPY OF YOUR RECEIPT TO:
JIM@HMODADDY.COM

PREFACE

I not only want to answer readers' questions, but also provide an insight into the topics asked. There are plenty of bland sites out there which give information. What I find landlords want is what to make of the facts: What other Landlords think about it, how much importance to attach to certain things or the value thereof. I must be careful with what I say as I do not want to be accused of inciting people to break the law or creating dissention.

The legislation aimed at the HMO property market is over 99% unnecessary and very badly or vaguely drafted. It is not based on any risk analysis but mainly a wish to control and restrict HMOs and persecute Landlords. The law is selectively enforced and mostly ignored. The reason the law is mainly ignored is often that those whose duty it is to enforce the law recognise this and wish to encourage the provision of housing so are disinclined to be over officious; also because they lack the resources. There are people, who for a salary, will enthusiastically enforce pointless rules, criminalise landlords and incur them in pointless expense.
I have made a number of YouTube videos on prepay meters. Please refer to the back page for links.

I hope my answers help, and please keep your questions coming as I enjoy helping you.

Question 1

Why did you fit prepay electric meters?

About 25 years ago I started fitting prepay meters. The reason for this was to stop tenants abusing the supply of free, inclusive electricity. I found that by fitting prepay meters in the HMO's the electric used decreased by up to 50%. Tenants' behavior changed overnight.

Before fitting prepay meters, when I went into any of my HMOs, many of the tenants would leave everything in their rooms switched on. After prepay meters were fitted, they would leave nothing switched on.

There is also the benefit of increasing the income from the HMO. I find that the meters not only reduced the cost of electric, but their income from the prepaid meters substantially reduced (and can even eliminate) the cost of providing electricity. It should also be appreciated that by reducing energy usage, you are doing your bit towards saving the planet.

Question 2

Why are you changing to Metro Prepaid meters?

I have recently started to fit Metro Prepaid meters www.metroprepaid.co.uk because they are cheap compared to conventional prepay meters, and very convenient for our tenants to use. Tenants can top up their meters online, by phone or from shops that offer PayPoint facilities. They also provide us with a monthly account of payments made. So far, apart from running extension leads to the communal supplies, we have not found any way staff or tenants can defraud us using Metro Prepaid meters. The meters are largely tamperproof. With the card meters, cash is often involved, if card meter cards go missing and the cards can be sourced from other suppliers. I have even had an ex-employee selling electric cards to my tenants at a discount.

The downside is that the Metro Prepaid meters take 9.55%+VAT for managing the account and payment takes up to a month to be made.

Question 3
Are properties with prepay meters harder to let?

I find my tenants prefer not to have prepay electric meters fitted into their rooms. They would rather pay me £10 a week more in rent.

We all have ideas, concepts or beliefs in our head which are difficult to shift. I probably more than most. I would ask you to reconsider your outright rejection of prepay meters. I have no vested interest in this apart from I fit and have fitted prepaid meters for almost 20 years. I get no money out of promoting prepay meters. No one is giving me commission for promoting their meters. What I do is share with other landlords my experience which is that the cost of electricity to the landlord almost halves when prepay meter when prepay meters are fitted to each tenant's room. Why? Because tenants change their behaviour, the tenant is now directly paying for the electric they use. Instead of many tenants leaving everything switched on, everything is switched off in their room. It stops tenants abusing the free supply of electric and you are also doing your bit to save the planet. The greenest energy is the energy not used.

I introduced prepay meters to stop tenants leaving electric heaters running 24/7 in their rooms and leaving windows wide open because, as one said to me, "They like fresh air and they also like to be warm!". I was not initially interested in the income obtained from prepay meters and I would give away the electric cards almost like confetti. (I now use online methods of payment with prepay meters I use which makes the administration and collecting payment much easier). I was just happy to save about 50% on my electric bill.

The massive increase in electric prices has changed things. Landlords have found their electric bills have increased from about 15p per kilowatt to 75p kilowatt. An increase of five times! I calculate the average tenant's electric usage will increase by £10 per week. This means that a six-bedroom HMO will cost at least £60 a week more to operate just on the electric never mind the gas!

NB from observation I find there is little variation in the utility costs between a three room and eight room HMO. This could be rationalised on the basis that a 3 or 8 room property may not vary that much in size, so the number of occupants makes little difference. The other issue I have is utility costs can vary enormously between HMOs, I can find little consistency, only an average.

I note you mention that your tenants would rather pay £10 a week more in rent than to have prepay electric meters. I agree, I calculate the average tenant's electric cost will increase by about £10 per week. This increase in cost will destroy many HMO businesses unless something is done to control the cost. On top of this is the massive increase in gas prices. To cover the increased cost in gas and electric I guess estimates that the landlord will have to charge their tenants and extra £20 a week. If the tenants are prepared to pay this then all is well and good. My experience is that few tenants will or can pay and I find using prepay meters the best alternative.

The use of prepay meters as I mentioned above is also environmentally beneficial and more fairly distributes the cost of electric between the tenants who use it and those who do not.

I have written a book on fitting prepay meters in HMOs entitled, "Everything you Need to Know About Fitting Prepay Meters in HMOs". It can be obtained as a free download or as a paid for book only at www.hmodaddy.com.

Question 4

Will prepay meters cause tenants to leave?

I do not personally know anyone that is fitting prepay meters in my area and looking on SpareRoom and other places where property is advertised, no one else is doing it either. What I have found in my area is that if you do something different people do not respond well to it.

As I have said, I have not had anyone refuse to take a room because it has a prepay meter fitted, but then they may not approach me if they know I have prepaid meters. I have a 30-room HMO all metered in your area without any issues and in good demand.

The main advantage of fitting prepay electric meters is not the income, but it reduces the electric bill for the landlord to the property by nearly 50%. Tenants' behaviour changes – instead of leaving everything switched on they switch everything off.

Question 5

Will I no longer have to pay for electricity when prepay meters are fitted?

It does not mean you do not have to pay for electric supplied to the HMO. The landlord pays for the electric into the property and this bill must be paid. Income from the prepaid meters will be added to the income produced by the property, like additional rent or having an extra room. You will still be paying for the electric for the communal areas but the cost of electric will be offset by the income produced by the meters. We meter each lettable room and the tenant pays for the electric in their own room.

By law, landlords are not allowed to make a profit on the resale of electric used by the tenant but can recover the cost of electric, standing charges and any administration costs. The landlord will still have to pay for the electric used in the communal areas. However, for 30 years I have analysed the electric, gas and water usage in my HMOs and the income from prepay electric meters and I find enormous variability, for which I am unable to identify the cause. Some properties use a lot more electricity or produce more income from prepay meters than others for no identifiable reason.

Question 6
Is it legal for Landlords to fit electricity prepay meters?

The fitting of sub meter or prepay meters is perfectly legal. I and other landlords have been doing it for decades. What a landlord cannot do is advertise their HMO as being fully inclusive when the tenant has to pay for the electric or heating. I get around this by advertising 'most bills are included'. The only restriction on charging for electric is that you are not allowed to make a profit out of the resale of electric, though you are allowed to recover all costs. The recovery of all costs is rather vague and could be interpreted to mean you could include a contribution towards the cost of installing and maintaining the meters and the cost of communal electricity.

For how to persuade your existing tenants to allow prepay meters to be fitted see Question and Answer 9.

Question 7

What can you charge for electricity when using prepay meters?

With prepay meters, you set the charges as you wish but by law you are not allowed to make a profit. For fairness, I keep the charge for electric at less than the highest tariffs being offered by suppliers, which is currently over 50p per kilowatt (January 2023). The lowest charge is about 20p per kilowatt but there are high standing charges at the cheapest rates, so it makes the actual cost of electricity per kilowatt difficult to calculate. Currently (January 2023) there is a residential cap of 35p per kilowatt.

Question 8

I know electricity companies are not allowed to turn off the supply of electric to residential occupiers. Would using a prepay meter be seen as disconnecting the supply for a tenant, if they are unable to pay?

If a tenant fails to maintain sufficient credit on the meter, then they effectively disconnect themselves and this is permissible. Landlords are not permitted to disconnect a tenant, for example, cutting the supply to the room or property if the tenant does not pay their rent even if the utilities are included. I appreciate it is a subtle distinction and the effect is the same as the tenant no longer has electricity, but one way is legal the other is not. What utility companies are allowed to do but a landlord CANNOT do is to fit prepay meters and recover outstanding debt by charging an amount every week. Utility companies can in my experience charge as much as £20 per week to recover utility debts.

A landlord CANNOT also recover any rent arrears via an electric prepay meter. The only way rent arrears can be recovered is through the courts if the tenant refuses to pay. See my manual 'DIY Eviction' only available from HMO Daddy via www.hmodaddy.com for more information on how to legally, quickly, simply and cheaply evict a tenant.

Question 9

When fitting a prepay meter, it is expected that tenants will have a given amount of electricity per month, or do they pay for all the electric they use?

We usually get the tenant to pay for all electric and no allowance is given. It is only when we introduce meters to an existing tenant who objects that we give anything. One of the ways of persuading them to allow a meter to be fitted is to give them a one-off credit of £20 to start with. With new tenants, no allowance is usually given unless we house contractors and their company is paying, in which case we keep their meters topped up.

Another way to persuade an existing tenant to allow a meter to be fitted is to give them a choice of £10-£20 a week rent increase or have a meter fitted. They always opt for having a meter fitted.

Question 10

How do tenants pay when a Metro Prepaid meter is fitted? Can this be done at the meter, online, or do they need to approach the landlord?

The big advantage of fitting Metro Prepaid meters over other brands is the administration of selling electricity is done by Metro Prepaid meters. The tenant can pay online, direct to Metro Prepaid meters or go to any PayPoint outlet.

Metro Prepaid meters do all the administration by sending the landlord a monthly account, a month in arrears, which shows each individual meter in the property and what has been paid by the tenant.

Question 11
Do tenants abuse the meters?

Unfortunately, albeit very occasionally, some tenants bypass the meter or run extension leads from the communal areas to steal electricity.

When I catch tenants running extension leads, I will remove them and leave a note stating that they are stealing electric (see page 37), and if they want the extension lead back then they will have to see me. I have obtained a lot of extension leads by this means and no one has ever asked for their extension lead back.

Tenants who are bypassing the meter usually leave everything switched on. If you go into a room when the tenant is not there and find electric appliances switched on, then 99% of the time you will find they have run an extension lead or bypassed the meter to avoid paying for the electricity. Another way to identify fraud is to monitor the amount of electric sold to each room, though I find there is a large variation in the amount of electric purchased by tenants.

Question 12

Do you have to buy electric from Metro Prepaid meters?

No, you are to choose our own supplier. I scour the market for the cheapest supplier and I have never found anyone who can do better, when the standing charges are factored in, but please let me know about your competitive supplier. I set the rate for which I resell the electric to the tenant and Metro Prepaid meters process the payment from the tenant to me.

Question 13

What do prepay meters cost to buy?

Card and coin prepay meters cost about £140 each (I get my card and coin meters from PJ Wales - 01626368595). Metro Prepaid meters (MET001 single phase meter) that I use costs around £60 including VAT.

For suppliers visit www.metroprepaid.co.uk.

Always try to negotiate a price with your supplier.

Metro Prepaid meters are so much cheaper to buy because they are selling them at close to cost to encourage sales. I believe that their strategy is to make money in the long term from recurring charges in administering the purchase of electricity through the meters. Also, Metro Prepay meters are fully digital and many call them SMART so they are cheaper to produce than the old coin meters with their mechanical components.

Question 14

Will the use of electricity meters deter potential new tenants?

It may do but we have had no experience of it deterring tenants. Although, we would be unaware as the tenants would not come and apply for accommodation if they know we charge them separately for electricity, i.e. bills are not all inclusive.

We occasionally get asked what the electricity would cost and if it is a room we tell them it will not cost much unless the tenant uses an electric heater or has a fridge or cooker.

I do not meter the electric light for safety reasons and there is very little else which uses much electric unless the tenant uses an electric heater. The electricity used by a phone, laptop charge or TV is very little.

Question 15

Are landlords doing enough to conserve energy?

Let us take a step back and ask does energy conservation work? I would like to do my bit to save the planet and at the same time save on my heating costs. I have tried numerous energy consumption measures in the 140 HMOs I operate where I provide 24/7 heating and hot water. Unlike most landlords I keep a weekly log of the energy used in each HMO by taking the meter readings and I cannot identify any change in the energy used before and after fitting conservation measures.

To give an example, I took out 30-year-old boilers, which could have easily been repaired, and fitted an A rated boiler because I was told they were up to 40% more efficient. After replacing the boiler, I found there was no change. So how can an A rated boiler be up to 40% more efficient? I can only say what works in practice for me and very little does. One thing that I find substantially saves energy costs is fitting prepay electric meters as using prepay meters halves the cost of the electric consumption in my HMOs. The greenest energy is the energy you do not use. A 50% energy reduction will be any landlord's best contribution to saving the planet. Another way to save energy costs is by putting the heating on a timer. I find that having the heating on for only eight hours a day instead of 24/7 saves about 30% but upsets my tenants. For more on energy conservation see Questions 20 to 26.

Am I doing something wrong or does energy consumption not work in practice?

Question 16

What happens if my electric company undercharges me?

If you have underpaid, then the electric company can back charge you but they can only go back 12 months. If this happens then negotiate a 12-month payment plan so, in effect, you are delaying payment even further. If you compare it to buying things on credit cards where you get charged about 30% interest, then every year the company does not charge you, you are saving 30% or even more as they can usually only go back 12 months and if they do, if you ask you can have up to 12 months to pay so at a 30% interest rate you are effectively only paying 59p in the £1.

Question 17
Why is the electric bill so low in my HMO?

Keep quiet and do not complain. I monitor the gas and electric used in my HMOs by reading the meters every week. The usage in HMOs varies considerably with some using double what others use with no rational reason. With the low usage properties, I just count my blessings. In the properties which have high usage I try and find ways to reduce costs.

Question 18

How can prepay meters save on heating costs?

The way I can eliminate the cost of supplying heating in my HMOs is to fit electric heaters in each room. If you are only providing electric heaters then they have to be fixed. You can fit electric radiators/panel heaters, but I prefer to fit fan heaters that can be attached to the wall as they can be fitted high up so will not so easily get damaged or have soft furnishings pushed against them, which can happen with electric radiators/panel heaters.

If there is central heating in the property, I tell my potential tenants and it is also in my tenancy agreement that the central heating is not a contractual obligation on me as the landlord to provide and if it is provided it is either to be paid for by the tenants directly or only provided at the landlord's discretion. For how to handle existing tenants see question 9.

Providing you have provided a fix form of heating for your tenants and you are not telling your tenants that you are providing 24/7 central heating the cost of heating is down to the tenant. There is nothing in law that says the landlord must pay for the tenant's heating. There is some vague legislation that says that the heating must be affordable but this probably is mainly applicable to single lets. Like so much in this business the rules are not clear-cut and very much depends on interpretation.

I do not want my HMOs to become damp and mouldy so I provide background heating. I state in the contract with my tenants that where central heating is fitted, it is not contractual obligation for the landlord to pay for, the central heating, it is provided at the landlords' discretion. This gets round the problem of tenants demanding the heating be on 24/7 even in the middle of a heat wave so they can dry their clothes on the radiator. In practice when tenants have to pay for something they rarely use it. Like kitchens in most of my HMOs, the heaters are not used because the tenants have to pay. As regards to kitchens the tenants do not have to pay to use the kitchen in my HMOs but most of my tenants do not cook. How and what they eat after 30 years of being an HMO landlord I have yet to discover.

Question 19

What is the cost and benefit of fitting secondary electric meters to each HMO room compared with having the utility supplier fit a separate supply to each room?

If you wish to charge each tenant for the electric they use in their room, then you can fit secondary prepay meters which can be Metro Prepaid, credit, coin or card operated. The landlord pays for the supply to the house and resells the electric to the tenants by collecting the money from the prepay meters if coin operated or by selling the tenant's electric cards. This is the cheapest way of installing a prepay system but may have the hassle of emptying the coin meters and the security issues involved. Card meters unlike coin meters do not often get broken into, but all electric meters can easily be bypassed. The tenants can use electric without paying for it and in effect putting the cost on to the landlord as the landlord is paying for the supply to the house

The cost of wiring up a room to use secondary meters depends on how it is done. There are two ways of doing it:

1. The cheapest method is to spur off the existing circuit in the room, usually from an existing socket blanking off the existing sockets and add new sockets. This costs me in labour and materials about £160 plus the cost of the secondary meter which cost about £20 for a credit meter, £120 for a card meter, and coin meters cost slightly less than card meters. Then there is the cost of the cards for the card meters which are about 20p each. Alternatively, as I am now doing, you can use Metro Prepay meters which cost about £60 each. As Metro Prepay meters are paid online, by phone or via Pay Point (a payment service) selling cards or emptying coin meters is eliminated.

2. To put each room on a separate circuit this involves fitting each room with a consumer unit and wiring back to a distribution board. The cost of this would depend on the number of electric points in the room but would be in the region of £500 per room plus the cost of the secondary meter (costs above).

To have each room provided with its own separate power supply by the power company is not something I have done. The last time I enquired to do this it cost in the region of £2K per supply or room depending on the distance from the supply. I was recently quoted £15K to fit an additional supply into a property. Then there is the cost of wiring up each room which is a similar cost as (2) above. However, by providing each room with its own power supply the risk of non-payment due to fraud is down to the power company. Where I have managed properties which have their own supply paid directly to the power companies, we have experienced enormous difficulties in getting the supply transferred to the new tenant and even lost tenants due to the problems of transferring the supply. There are no such problems with using secondary meters.

Question 20

How do you manage your utilities so they do not get out of hand?

I have the gas, electric and water meters read weekly. I set a weekly average per occupant of 20 units (kwatt) of electric, three units (cubic meters) of gas and where the water is metered one cubic meter of water per person. Appreciate I do not have any HMOs with less than five tenants. If it was a small HMO I would expect greater usage to cover communal costs. So, for a six-bed HMO I would expect no more than 120 units of electric, 18 units of gas and 6 cubic meters of water to be used in a week. Anything in excess or out of the normal would result in investigation.

One of the costliest faults I have found is when someone leaves a hot tap running. Something as minor as this can cost you over £100 per week in extra cost for water and gas. It only has to be a steady trickle and the water and gas usage (all my water is heated by gas) goes through the roof. At least if you check it weekly you can quickly put a stop to any excess use.

Question 21
Would you be better off having a water meter fitted to your HMO?

I have two of my HMOs fitted with water meters and have found that each tenant uses around about £20 per month.

I would never have a water meter fitted in my property as in my experience the cost of water is over twice, sometimes far more than an unmetered supply. In one instance I had a bill of nearly £1,000 extra when a tenant broke the water pipe and flooded the cellar. Not only did I have the flood to contend with, but it resulted in dry rot.

Even on your calculations a 5-bed HMO would cost £1200 pa compared to my average water rates of about £300pa or £5 per month per tenant and no risk of excess charges should a leak occur.

Question 22

What energy efficiency measures do you recommend I follow?

Other than fitting prepay meters, none! Energy efficiency is a con!

I feel like I am the soldier marching correctly and everyone else is out of step over this. Energy efficiency measures, in my experience, do nothing to save anything in the cost of heating an HMO property where the landlord provides 24/7 central heating. I pay for the heating in the 140 HMOs I operate and I am perhaps in a position that most landlords are not, in that I measure the energy usage so I can compare the results over a large number of properties. I find the energy efficiency measures I have had installed have had no bearing on the cost of heating nor does the age of the building make any difference. I have tried roof and wall installation, double glazing, energy efficient boilers and energy efficient lighting.

I should add that I provide 24/7 central heating in most of my HMOs. Yes, you will save heating costs by switching off the heating when it is not needed. A long time ago I had a system in my HMOs where the heating was only on for eight hours a day and the saving was about a third over having the heating on 24/7, a significant saving but not proportionate to the time the heating is used. If the cost of heating was proportionate I would have saved two thirds of the cost.

Before the rise in energy costs, gas heating cost on average £1,600 pa for an HMO of up to eight rooms. This means I would save about £500 pa or £10 pw by limiting the heating to eight hours a day. However, some tenants will object and it's likely some will leave. I find tenants demand 24/7 heating and so do some housing officers. Keep switching the heating on and off does not save that much. The reason is that it probably costs a lot to heat the property back up. Compare a saving of £10pw to tenant dissatisfaction and losing tenants, it is not I believe worth the saving.

There are systems that can switch radiators off when the room is not in use or when the window is opened but as heating cost is not proportionate to the time the heating is on, I doubt these systems will save very much compared to their cost. The same goes for systems which switch off the heating if the property is empty, unless the property is empty for hours.

32

When it comes to switching heating on and off I believe, but I have not done any research on this, it is only observation, that the type of house is significant. A new well insulated house will heat up very quickly and also lose heat very quickly if a door of window is open. In a new house, I have not tried it, but I believe significant saving can be achieved by switching off if the property is empty for more than, and I am only guessing, an hour. With old solid brick houses they take hours to cool down and to heat up so there is no point switching off the heating unless the house is going to be empty for and again, I am guessing, 6 hours and you need to allow a few hours for the heating to warm the house up.

I believe Landlord Associations should research this and if my findings are the same then the associations should be screaming from the rooftops that carrying out energy efficiency measures will not save energy costs. It is wasting landlord's money. This con needs to be exposed.

There are four things, apart from limiting the time the heating is on, that I find will save money in heating and they are:

1. The cheapest and easiest is to shop around for the cheapest utility supplier. This can reduce your energy bills by up to 50%.

2. Fit prepay electric meters to each room. This means the tenants pay directly for the electric they use in their room. My experience is that the amount of electric used drops by nearly 50% when tenants have to pay for their electric. On average saving £400 pa on an HMO with up to 8 rooms. (This figure is pre the enormous rise in energy). Also, you can recover some or even all of the cost of the electric supplied by charging the tenants for the electric.

3. Do NOT fit gas or pay for central heating. This saves the cost of heating the property, around about £1,600 pa and with the enormous increase in utility prices possibly a lot more for up to an 8 room HMO. However, doing this is fraught with difficulties. For example: the property will probably fail an EPC if it has not got central heating fitted (oddly, if central heating is fitted it does not have to be used) and be cold and damp, unappealing for tenants and cause tenants to leave.

4. Fit undersized gas boilers to the property. This will only work in a large HMO or if you can link two or more HMOs together on one boiler.

33

Providing there is a thermostat fitted the small boiler will use less gas than a larger capacity boiler so save cost.

I would love to be proved wrong over my views on energy consumption as I desperately would love to save cost on utilities. Unfortunately, everything I have tried apart from 1 to 4 above has not worked or been viable in practice.

Question 23

Which energy conservation method do you recommend Jim?

This is one where I am nearly always disbelieved. I have tried a number of energy saving strategies such as the installation of loft and wall insulation, double glazing and energy efficient boilers. None of these has made any difference to the utility bills. The amount of gas used to heat the property has remained the same as it did before. I provide 24/7 gas powered central heating in most of my HMOs and so I expected to see a significant saving from these measures. I could also go on about light timers, LED bulbs and energy-efficient electric heaters, which led to little or no difference in electricity consumption.

Insulation does have benefits such as reducing condensation and mould, increasing the comfort of a property and reduces noise, but it does not save me money in energy costs.

Question 24

I have been recommended to change my gas central heating boiler for a new energy efficient one. What is your view on this?

Please do not get me going about gas central heating boilers! Always repair an old boiler if you can, as in my experience new boilers do not save any money in running costs and breakdown very easily. New boilers are not as reliable and robust as the old boilers and I suspect even if the old boiler is over twenty years old it will still outlast a new boiler, providing you can get the parts for them. A few years ago my old boilers broke down, I replaced them with the new energy efficient boilers. I then found I had to replace the new boilers within about two years, so I stopped doing this. I also found that they did not save any money in running costs even though they are advertised as being 40% more efficient.

New boilers, if over pressured, are easily damaged beyond repair and must be replaced. Tenants are in the habit of messing with the boilers and have wrecked nearly every new boiler I have fitted by over pressuring them. I would ignore what the advertising says about energy efficient boilers and stick to the old boiler that is fitted if you can. If you have to replace the boiler, then fit it in such a way that the tenants cannot interfere with it and get one with a long guarantee. What the suppliers do not tell you about is the extra 'free' guarantee that the manufactures give is that the boiler will not last much longer than it is guaranteed to last. The only downside I have found is that having an old boiler can affect your EPC rating, but I would still strongly recommend you not to change an old boiler for a new boiler unless you have to.

Question 25

What do you make of energy conservation measures?

I have 140 HMO's where I pay for the utilities and I have tried every type of conservation measure. I find they make no difference to the amount of gas and electricity that I use. The only thing that is true about conservation is the first three letters, it is a massive con, probably bigger than credit card fraud, misselling of PPI and the misselling of mortgage securities that lead to the financial crash in 2008.

What I find amazing is that whenever I mention this, particularly within council circles who I believe realise this massive con, no one will speak out and generally remain remarkably silent about implementing energy conservation measures in housing. They hold themselves out as highly principled people that are on the side of tenants and boast about how they have targeted bad landlords, yet there is this massive fraud going on around them, which totally eclipses the harm caused by any bad landlord.

Question 26

Have you tried any of the measures to conserve energy, such as fitting LED bulbs?

I have fitted LED bulbs and can detect no difference in electric consumption. Energy efficient bulbs now cost very little if you shop around (try Poundland) so even though I had to pay for them I am not upset and I only replaced the bulbs with LED as the old ones burnt out.

I have come to the conclusion that there is a massive flaw in the conservation argument and that is: insulation does not work in HMOs when providing 24/7 central heating. I am not saying that energy conservation does not work in other types of houses as I do not have any evidence apart from my own houses but I do have my doubts. What works in an HMO where 24/7 central heating is required is to restrict the supply or have the tenants pay for the cost of heating directly.

To come up with a workable system in a multi let house you have to get the tenants to agree to pay for the central heating and they have to coordinate as a group. Where the tenants are not a cohesive group which is the case with all my HMOs, they will not agree how to share the cost of heating and it will lead to disharmony. The only way to create responsibility for heating a house where the tenants are not a group is to charge the tenants individually which means not using central heating and fitting electric heaters to each room with each room being fitted with a prepay meter. This eliminates the cost to the landlord of heating the house and as the tenants have to pay, they rarely use the electric heaters.

Human behaviour is consistent, provide more food and people will overeat, provide more alcohol and they will drink more alcohol and so on. With heating it appears if the cost does not trouble the tenant, which it will not if the landlord is paying, they will just use more heating. As I have said, the only thing that seems to work is to limit the supply of energy or directly charge the tenants.

As previously mentioned, I will not try the various systems such as the window system where if you open a window the radiator in the room will switch off because I believe the savings will not pay for the cost of installation and maintenance. I will, however, be keen to know the experience of others, just in case I am wrong. What I find disheartening is landlords do not do very much empirical analysis of such matters as the saving in the cost of energy. The standard reply I get from landlords who uses energy saving measures is it must work because the advertising says so or logic says it does but they are unable to produce any evidence to show they compared the before and after figures.

Unfortunately, the figures based on my research do not show any worthwhile or cost-effective savings from any of the conservation measures so far but I would like to find and would implement energy saving measures that work.

Question 27

Does anyone use thermostats such as Hive, Nest, Inspire, Time:O:Start, etc?

Can you move these systems to another property as in re-wire it into another property? I ask as I am debating whether to buy one for a Rent-to-Rent property I will be giving back in a years' time. My tenants leave the heating on 24/7 and when it gets too hot they put fans on and open the windows.

The question you should be asking about Hive, Genius etc is will it save you very much money or even any money after you have added back the cost of buying and installing the equipment and your time in monitoring it. I very much doubt you will save anything worthwhile and upset the tenants in the meantime, as they dislike the heating being switched off.

Even though I think you will waste your time, I would very much like you to try any of these systems out, provided you keep the before and after records of the energy used in your HMO, so you can evidence the savings. All the people I have spoken to who have used these systems, just automatically assumed it saves money without checking to see if it did.

What does seem to change behavior is to stick a notice on the window saying, 'Please keep closed, save energy and the planet'. I will send you a copy, just email me at jim@hmodaddy.com These only costs 10p to make and hopefully achieve your objective.

Question 28

As a landlord what are you doing to save energy and help save the planet?

I have looked into saving energy not only to save the planet, if you believe it needs saving, but let's not get into that debate, but as a Scot, I also like to save money and as energy conservation can also save money, I have explored it and spent tens of thousands of pounds or should I say wasted tens of thousands of pounds trying out the so-called conservation strategies. However, unlike many or should I say anyone I have come across, I have monitored before and after performance and I am in an almost unique position to do this with over one hundred properties where I pay for the gas and electric and I monitor the utility usage of my HMOs on a weekly basis. My experience is that fitting energy efficient boilers, wall insulation and roof insulation saves very little and mostly nothing. As I do not believe my own experience with roof insulation and because it is often free or cheap to do, I continue to fit roof insulation. It does not usually hurt to fit insulation and the need to do so is or becoming mandatory. I find the same about insulation for immersion heaters, I can detect no saving but still insulate. I however, I bitterly regret replacing 20 to 30-year-old boilers instead of repairing them for very little compared to the cost of replacing them, for a so-called energy efficient boiler, which mostly had to be replaced after about a year.

I should emphasise that I am not an expert in this area but seem to know more than many who promote or sell these conservation systems or do energy surveys. I suggest and it is only a suggestion as I have no evidence or research to support this view, that unless the house is sealed like a Tupperware box and has heat exchangers fitted then insulation or efficient boilers save very little. When you speak to energy assessors they just reply, 'The book says' and this is after we have sent half our population to university. I thought the idea of education was to get people to think and reason for themselves! I suspect the assessors know or suspect there is something very wrong but it suits them financially not to know that energy efficiency measures do not work in practice.

The fact that nobody else seems to have realised that insulation is not working is a puzzle to me and I wonder if it is anything to do with the government wanting to achieve energy reduction targets that the truth is suppressed? Why are people who know not also speaking out? Why, like fire sprinklers, is it that it only seems to be me who is telling the truth? I have sadly come to a conclusion that energy conservation is a con and those peddling it are charlatans. Ask yourself why the Green Deal sank without trace? The only way I believe to save energy in a house is at the build stage or by undertaking massive adaptions to an existing house. For energy conservation to work the house has to have good insulation, be sealed and depending on its layout a two-door entry and exit system, where one door has to be closed before the other is opened to prevent too much heat being lost entering and exiting the building and a ventilation system where the incoming outside cold air gets heated by the warm, expelled foul air.

A sealed ventilation system is where the warm stale air in the house is used to heat the incoming air. When the property is being heated you cannot open a window. It is, I believe all or nothing. In a house which does not have a sealed ventilation system then the very best roof insulation or other insulation just lets the heat out elsewhere. If there is a hole in the house e.g. an open window door or vent, the heat will just flow out of it.

I think the position is even worse, with the houses built in the last twenty years the internal insulation of walls has stopped the capability of the brick walls to store heat if it has brick walls. Open a door or window and the heat just flows out. With old brick built houses the heat is absorbed by the brick walls and is stored for a long time, so it takes hours to cool down and to heat up. The house itself is like an enormous electric storage heater. I find that old houses, if kept warm costs less to keep warm than a modern house. Following this logic external cladding of walls in old houses should work but I can find no savings. Perhaps brick walls do not transmit very much heat or it causes the heat to bounce back into the house and flow out of any open door, window or vent.

In other words, providing you wish to keep the house warm 24/7 an old house is actually cheaper to heat than a modern house. Possibly a modern house becomes much cheaper to heat if the heating is used only occasionally as it uses less energy to warm up and holds the heat better than an old house providing no one opens a door or window. I cannot verify this hypothesis as I have not tried it but I live in a modern house, and I note how quickly it warms up compared to my Victorian built HMOs.

I find my modern HMO houses cost me more to heat than my old HMO houses. This may be due to me having a policy of keeping the heating on 24/7. Unfortunately, some of the tenants often leave open the doors or windows because they complain it is too hot and are incapable of turning down radiators. I have therefore, concluded that this is down to new houses not holding the heat in their walls. I will try when I get time install devisees which limit the heating i.e. using Hive or an occupation detector which turns the heating off if the house is unoccupied to see if this makes any difference.

Do not despair, there are two ways you can save over 50% on your gas and electric bills. Firstly, if you have not already done it, by shopping around for the cheapest supplier. The difference in cost between the most expensive and cheapest suppliers are over 50%. Secondly, you can save a further 50% on your electric cost by fitting pre-paid meters to your tenant's rooms. When the tenants pay directly for their electricity they ensure everything is switched off when not being used.

Question 29

How do you save money on gas and electricity?

I would love to know how to save more on gas and electricity. I have written on the subject a number of times. In my experience what I find saves significantly on electric, but is the second-best way to save on electric is to fit prepay electric meters to each room. You can use coin meters but I do not for security reasons. The tenant purchase cards from us (usually costing £5) though I have recently changed to fitting Metro Prepaid meters where the electric can be purchased online and at any Pay Point outlet so removing the need to supply electric cards and substantially reduce the analysis and accounting time involved as Metro Prepaid meters produce a monthly analysis.

I find when meters are fitted the electric usage in the whole property almost halves compared to the electric the property previously used. If you fit prepay meters you need to be observant and check the tenants are buying electric cards and are not by-passing the meter (easy to do and it is where the tenant loops out the electric meter so they get free electric) or using extension leads to steal electricity from the communal areas. NB an alternative to prepay meters is credit meters. These measure how much electricity is used (they are cheaper to buy but how effective they would be in reducing electric use I do not know as I have never tried them) but they avoid the need to supply cards for the prepay meters. However, you will be left with the problem of getting the tenants to pay and possible arguments about the accuracy of the meter.

If we discover the tenant has by-passed the meter or is using an extension lead to steal electric from the communal areas, we give them an official warning, explain it is a criminal offence and charge them £50. We tell the tenant if they do it again we will report them to the police and ask them to leave and if they do not leave we evict them. The tenants then behave or we evict them for non-payment of rent as stealing electric and non-payment of rent always goes together. If the tenant is out and I discover an extension lead, I remove it leaving a note as above (see page 34) but saying that they can collect the lead from the office. So far, no one has asked for their extension lead back.

The easiest way to save on electricity is by using the cheapest supplier.

The cost of electric can vary between suppliers by 300%. However, it is very difficult to compare costs of electric when you take into account the standing charges. The cheapest per kw is not the overall cheapest when standing charges are taken into account. Average use for a six room HMO, for me, is about 120 kw per week. For reasons I do not understand, I find landlords are very reluctant to change suppliers and the same goes for insurance, yet good savings can easily be made by doing both.

The traditional way I was taught to save on electric, is by going around switching off lights but this does not seem to make any difference, though I still do it. I fit energy efficient bulbs and I know theoretically they should save but again I can detect no measurable difference in the electric used in a house after I have changed the bulbs. This is probably because lighting is not that expensive. The majority of the cost of electric is heating, be it water or space heating and washing machines though I find fridges also use a lot of power.

With gas, again the big saving is by going for the cheapest supplier. I cannot find a way you can charge individual tenants for gas central heating apart they pay a proportion of the bill. You could try a fair use policy but with the tenants I have, this would not work. With some we struggle to get them to pay the rent. If the tenants are a cohesive responsible group i.e. students or come together then a fair use policy may work.

The other two ways I find you can make an identifiable saving in gas heating costs is to fit a thermostat to the boiler (it is unusual to find a boiler without a thermostat fitted but it is worth checking). Fitting a thermostat can half the heating cost. The second is with semi-detached houses, linking boilers i.e. heat both houses using only one boiler saves between 20% and 40% on the previous heating costs. This also has the advantage that there is only one boiler to service. I do not upgrade the boiler; I use one of the existing boilers and I normally do this when one of the boilers breaks down and is beyond repair.

Apart from fitting a thermostat to the boiler and linking boilers, I do not know of any other way of reducing gas costs as dramatically as you can for electric. Ensuring there is a thermostat hidden away so tenants cannot alter it or its pre-set and the tenants can only turn the heating off and turning the controls down, does not, I find, save that much.

I cannot identify any savings between the before and after consumption of gas and electric after doing energy conservation measures. I have tried fitting insulation in the roof, wall insulation and installing energy efficient boilers. Please do not get me wrong, I would love to do my bit for the planet and save energy but being a bit of a pragmatist, I would like to see evidence and so far my experience has identified no savings. Where I have reduced ceiling heights in rooms and put insulation above, it makes the room more comfortable and soundproof but I have yet to compare, as I have with electric meters, the before and afterwards to see if it saves. Double glazing also makes the room and house more comfortable but I am not sure how much it saves. I am not saying that energy conservation measures do not have any benefit. I find as I have stated that they make the property more comfortable and may reduce mould spots but so far I cannot identify any cost saving.

I suspect with modern properties which are well insulated, turning the heating off probably using something like Hive or Nest would make savings as they are quick to heat up unlike an uninsulated house which takes time to heat but using Hive or Nest would require constant management and a way of knowing whether the property was occupied. If you turn the heating off when tenants are in occupation they will complain and possibly leave. I have yet to try timer switches where the heating switches off after a pre-set time and has to be manually turned back on by the tenants.

I find with old uninsulated properties turning the heating on and off does not save as much as you would expect. For example, having the heating on for two hours in the morning and five hours in the evening only saves less than 30%, a significant saving but results in great dissatisfaction from the tenants. Logically, you would think having the heating on for seven hours would save 70% in energy costs as it is only being used for less than a third of the day. I suspect the reason I only get less than a 30% saving is because it costs so much to heat the property back up again.

Whenever, I try to discuss how to save on heating costs with other landlords they never had any empirical evidence to back up what they save i.e. before and after figures. All I get from other landlords is bland replies like, 'Of course using X or Y saves money' or, 'The advertising says I will save'. Never do they have any figures to back up their assertions such as before or after figures. Their views are based on feelings.

As I continually try to explain, this business is not logical and the cost of electric, heating and water usage does not appear to follow a logical pattern. For example, I find it costs on average the same in utilities (council tax, gas, water and electric) for a four-bed house as it does for an eight-bed house. I know this because my staff read the gas, electric and water meters on a weekly basis and I compare costs. I have tried insulating my properties and fitting energy efficient boilers but I find it does not make any identifiable difference to my heating costs. The result of taking energy efficient measures may be a warmer or cooler house or any savings are lost by tenants opening the windows and let the heat out, either way, energy conservation does not translate into cost savings and if the house is not warm it leads to tenant dissatisfaction.

I have also tried not fitting central heating and fitting fixed electric heaters so putting the cost of heating onto the tenants by the use of prepay meters in each room. This has worked in houses which are naturally warm so eliminating the cost of central heating resulting in a substantial saving. However, with most houses without heating they are very cold and create a miserable environment. Lack of central heating also can cause problems with EPC (Energy Performance Certificate) ratings which now have to be a minimum of a 'E'. It is hard for a property without central heating to achieve an 'E' rating.

I struggle to find any consistency in heating costs between some like for like properties. With some, the heating costs are a third of a similar property but for no obvious reason that I can identify. Though if you are measuring consumption using gas units used, appreciate some old meters are cubic feet and modern ones are cubic meters. One property will be very hot yet costs a fraction of the cost of another similar property which is always cool. This is why I always, when testing energy consumption, I use a before and after measure not a similar property analysis and I accept even this is flawed as the usage as measured by meter reads for the previous year may not be the same for the following year. For example, last year may have been colder or warmer or there are different tenants in the house. However, it is the best guide I have and generally, heating costs in the same house are consistent year on year. Further, I find what are supposed to be well insulated new houses cost the same and sometimes more to heat than the old uninsulated houses.

I would love someone to spend time analysing my heating use and cost. I have employed people to do this who have assured me they can save me money on heating costs and have saved other businesses money but when I have asked them to show me the evidence i.e. reduced consumption as shown by my meter readings they have always been unable to show any evidence apart from saying, 'The book' or some association says it should make a saving. I even had one energy consultant take great offence saying even large companies had never demanded proof, they took his word that savings were made. Unfortunately, he was unable to make any saving for me though he spent a lot of time investigating.

The consultants I have used have been unable to give me any explanation why I get such diverse heating costs and even though they say they can save, for example, 'Up to 40%', seem surprised that I should demand proof. Now when approached by such consultants, I tell them I am not interested in what the figures say I will save or what they have allegedly saved others. I will only use their services if they agree that I need only pay them if they can provide evidence to prove to me they have saved me money and their service is cost effective.

I have yet to decide what I would pay to save on cost. For example, 10% of the saving or 50% in the first year? I think 50% of the saving in the first year would not be excessive if the savings were on going. Assuming the cost of energy remains the same over the ten years it would only cost me 5% of the total saving less cost of money over ten years. So far the consultants I have spoken to say they cannot guarantee that any saving will be made or I never hear back from them. I think it is best to assume all energy conservation methods, apart from what I have mentioned as working, are a con. They do not make any measurable cost saving.

I am fed up of hearing about theoretical savings such as fitting infra-red switches or timers to lights, mainly because the math's never stack up when I work them. For example, putting a timer on a 10-watt light even if it saves 50% on a 24/7 365-day basis, assuming KW of electricity costs 15p, it will only save £6-57 pa (24 hours' x 356 ÷ 1000/10 x 15p) yet costs the best part of £100 to install. Also, as I have said previously, I have changed to LED bulbs and can detect no measurable saving in the electric use compared to when the old less efficient bulbs were used.

To conclude, I am undecided whether energy efficiency does not work or does not work in practice. The answer is I suspect is that the tenants just

48

open the windows and let the heat out. If I am correct in my assumption, then the way to save on heating costs is to limit the amount of energy used in the first place rather than insulation. A difficult balancing act as the property needs to be kept warm otherwise this leads to tenant dissatisfaction but not warm enough that the tenants open the window to let the heat out. In other words only a modest amount of heat is allowed to be used but enough for the property to feel warm all the time.

If my hypotheses is correct and I emphasise it is only a conjecture, it explains why well insulated houses can cost more to heat. It is because, unlike uninsulated houses, they do not absorb the heat, so when a door or window opens the heat just pours out. With uninsulated houses they act like giant storage heaters, the walls absorb the heat and they cost more to warm up but once warmed up retain the heat.

What I cannot explain is the variation between similar houses in heating costs and electric unless it is that the meters are faulty.

SUMMARY			
ORDER	GAS	ELECTRIC	SAVING
TOP	Cheapest supplier	Cheapest supplier	Up to 65%
SECOND	Fit thermostat to boiler	Fit pre-pay meters	Up to 50%
THIRD	Link boilers	–	Up to 30%

I find no significant saving can be made by doing anything else. Switching off and conservation measures do not make any measurable difference.

Question 30

How do I fit prepay meters to a room?

Method 1

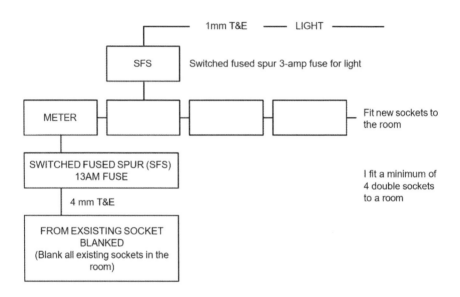

*Connect 4 mm T&E to anyone of your existing sockets provided it is on the ring main and blank off all the sockets in the room.
* T&E twin and earth electric cable, it is usually grey in colour.

1. Fit prepay meter at a convenient spot in the room no higher than 5 feet from the ground so that the card can be used without having to stand on a chair/ step. Some EHO officers consider it unsafe to have to use steps to access meters.

2. If you wish the light etc can be run off the meter by spurring off a new socket and fitting a switched fused spur installed with a 3amp fuse.

3. New digital card meters and the cards are obtainable from PJ Wales 01626368595 for about £140 each + VAT and P&P. The single use cards cost about 20p each and the multi-use cards about £1 each.

Metro Prepay meters can be obtained from most large electrical suppliers for about £60 + VAT each (for suppliers visit www.metroprepaid.co.uk).

Method 2 - Separate Circuit

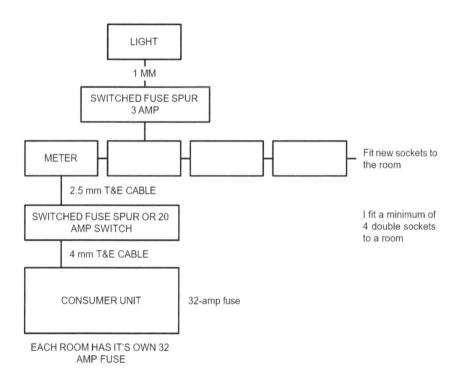

Question 31

How do tenants top-up Metro Prepaid meters?

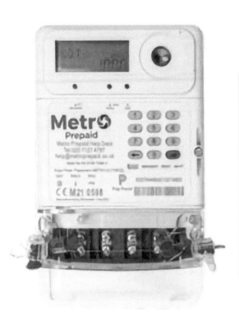

TOPPING THE METER UP

There will be a card that comes with the meter, take this card to a Pay Point shop, they will scan it and then give you a receipt that has a 20-digit code on, take this back to your meter and enter the number followed by enter key.

Sometimes if you do not type it in quick enough the screen will go off, to get the screen back on press any number, once the screen is back on carry on typing in the code.

TOPPING THE METER UP ON THE PHONE

Call Metro Pay-By-Phone and allow the voice prompts to guide you through the process of paying on your Visa or Mastercard debit or credit card.

Metro Pay-By-Phone can be contacted on 028 4142 4538

TOPPING UP WITHOUT CARD

If you do not have the card to your meter. The barcode that is on the card is also on the meter. Take your meter card, digital barcode, print-out of barcode or photo of barcode to any PayPoint out. The shop keeper should be able to use this.

If you cannot locate your barcode, please call Metro Prepaid Help Desk which is available 24/7 on 020 3020 1144

Question 32

Do you warn tenants who steal electricity?

Example:

It has been found that electricity has been used in your room without being paid for either by linking out the electric meter or by use of an extension lead.

It is a criminal offence to take electricity without payment for it and if it happens again we will be report it to the Police for prosecution.

You have been charged a nominal £50 towards the cost of:
(a)   serving this notice
(b)   electric taken
(c)   for the cost of rectifying the damage if any caused and as a deterrent.

If you have any explanation or excuse for what happened let me know. Landlord

Tenant: _____

Property: _____   Unit: _____

Date Discovered: _____   Time: _____

By: _____   Photographed: YES/NO

Details: _____

_____

_____

_____

_____

_____

Question 33

**I am a letting agent and I am thinking of suggesting my landlords fit prepay meters into their HMO's due to the number who are complaining about the utility costs. I am worried about what extra administration this would involve me in.
Your thoughts please?**

From past experience if you are going to do it, you have to do it right. There can be a lot of work involved in the administration of prepay meters and sorting out the income. If you had to employ another member of staff to do the administration it could cost more in staffing costs than the gross income from the meters. I can now begin to understand why when Letting Agents take over properties with prepay meters they often refuse to administer them and on occasions where I have been involved, they have asked me to remove them. My staff have to spend a considerable amount of time dealing with tenants who do not understand or choose not to understand how prepay meters work.

The main benefit of installing prepay meters is it limits the amount of electricity the tenants use and in my experience the electric bill, which the landlord pays on the property, almost halves overnight after prepay meters are installed. The tenant's behaviour changes from leaving everything switched on to switching everything off. In other words, they save the landlord money because the electricity used is almost halved, the income for me is secondary. For my own properties I am prepared to tolerate the inadequacy in the administration because I realise I am saving on the electricity but landlords do not take kindly to errors and the administration in dealing with them could be too much if it is not organised correctly.

What would avoid a lot of administration is if you used Metro Prepaid meters and have payments made direct to your landlord account. With Metro Prepaid meters, payment is made online, as opposed to other types which are coin operated so need emptying or card meters where cards are sold to the tenants to top up the meter. Using Metro Prepaid gets round the problem of you having to administer and account for the income. If the landlord wants you to monitor the income they could copy you into the account, so we could identify tenants who are not paying and investigate why and it would also highlight abnormal use.

For example, low income from the meters could indicate the tenants were bypassing them or running extensions from the communal areas. This is quite a common practice.

YouTube Links
Talks on Metro Prepaid meters

https://www.youtube.com/watch?v=WjtcQovw05I

https://www.youtube.com/watch?v=tLBZaFZMey8

https://www.youtube.com/watch?v=I_6aI66BRVM

https://www.youtube.com/watch?v=-cyzQqiBEEs

https://www.youtube.com/watch?v=iRhCSA9XygU

List of Publications

NO	BOOKS	PRICE	√
1	HMO Landlord Rules	£4-97	
2	50 Myths for HMO Landlord	£9-97	
3	Planning & HMOs		
4	HMOs & Compensation for Unlawful Eviction	£9-97	
5	101 Questions and Answer for HMO Landlords	£9-97	
6	Even More 101 Questions and Answer for HMO Landlords	£9-97	
7	35 Money Saving Tips for HMO Landlords	£9-97	
8	Serviced Accommodation	£9-97	
9	A Compendium of HMO Daddy Blogs	£9-97	
10	Introduction to Letting to The Unemployed	£9-97	
11	Current Issues for HMO Landlords	£9-97	
	MANUALS		
12	A Guide to Becoming a Multi-Millionaire HMO Landlord	£597	
13	DIY Eviction	£125	
14	Operating standards for HMO Landlords	£297	
15	Forms and Letters for HMO Landlords	£125	
16	How to Get Properties for Free (almost) and Turn Them into Money Making Machines	£297	

I wish to purchase the above books √:

NAME: ....

ADDRESS: ....

POSTCODE: ....

TEL: .... EMAIL: ....

PAYMENT:
CASH: £............ CHEQUE: £............ INVOICE: £............ CARD: £..............

Either email order to: jim@hmodaddy.com
Or
Send to: 14 Walsall Road, Wednesbury, WS10 9JL

Books, Manuals, Mentorship and Consultancy

BOOKS

HMO Landlord Rules - £ 4.99
Downloadable version - £1.99

Written by an HMO landlord with 20 years' experience, this small, frank and helpful guide looks at exactly what works and what doesn't when managing properties. Instilled with a strong sense of evidence and proof, he exposes some widely- accepted claims as rubbish or a con. The aim is to ensure maximum income for minimum work. It includes helpful information such as:

- How to pick good tenants and get rid of bad ones
- Whether to believe non-payment excuses
- When to give something for free and when to charge
- When to serve notice on a tenant
- How to deal with abandonment and late payments
- How to avoid litigation
- and much more a set of rules, principles and structure for all HMO Landlords.

50 Myths for HMO Landlords - £9.97
Downloadable version - £6.93

A list of the top 50 misconceptions about the HMO business. For example:

- You cannot get all your money and more out of a deal
- Energy conservation saves money
- Housing standards are of benefit
- Valuers can value
- You get what you pay for
- You need money to get into property
- It is hard to evict a tenant.

101 Questions & Answers relating to HMOs - £9.99
Downloadable version - £6.93

All the questions you wanted answers to and some you had not even thought about. Jim Haliburton, also known as the HMO Daddy, has compiled the answers to

the questions he has been asked. There is an enormous thirst for knowledge about HMOs from existing HMO landlords and those thinking of entering the business and HMO Daddy has not shirked away from answering even the most difficult of them. A must read for all those who have HMOs or are thinking about becoming an HMO landlord.

More 101 Questions & Answers relating to HMOs - £9.99
Downloadable version - £6.93

In this book, Jim Haliburton answers even more of the essential questions you wanted to know about HMOs including his personal property journey, how to get started on your HMO journey, potential tenant issues, how to let the unemployed or homeless, dealing with utilities, handing general HMO issues, matters regarding the authorities prosecuting landlords and HMO funding techniques.

35 Money Making or Saving Tips for HMO Landlords - £9.99
Downloadable version - £6.93

Written by an experienced HMO landlord, this is an insider's guide to creating extra income and savings from your property portfolio. It includes information to help you make savings on repairs, maintenance and decoration of your properties. It includes tried and tested tips used by the author himself, and includes information on creating extra rooms in your properties, introducing and charging extra fees and top-ups, fitting master locks and electric meters, making savings on light fittings, repairs and decoration. It explains which services can be charged for and which should be free, as well as how and when to introduce new fees without upsetting your tenants. If you're and HMO landlord, this will give you a frank and honest way to maximise the returns on your property. Just applying FIVE of the tips to four of your HMOs will give you the PROFIT of an EXTRA HMO.

Planning & HMOs - £9.99
Downloadable version -£6.93

HMO landlords provide low-cost flexible housing desperately needed by society, often to vulnerable tenants. However, they are rarely given help or support by the authorities, and the law is often vigorously enforced against them. Little is said about the damage some tenants cause to property, problems with rent arrears and eviction of bad tenants. This book is for the brave souls who dare to provide HMO housing and need a guide to the planning system. It shows you how to stand up to councils that try to stop you providing good quality HMO accommodation. If you stand up to the planners, you will be surprised how rarely they will flow through and how often they will lose. A unique insight and practical information about planning rules and planning appeals for shared houses and multi-lets by an experienced HMO landlord.

HMO & Compensation for Unlawful Eviction - £9.99
Downloadable version - £6.93

This practical, down to earth guide is written by HMO Daddy an experienced landlord who had a case brought against him for unlawful eviction by an HMO tenant. When he got to court, he realised he was looking at a possible compensation claim of around £100,000. With no experience in this area, he could find little guidance or help to explain the system. He won his case – but this is the book he wishes he'd had at the time! This quick and easy-to-understand guide examines court reports and cases involving unlawful eviction along with the amount of compensation awarded. It brings home to landlords, the seriousness of the risks they are taking when evicting tenants and more importantly it explains how to avoid ending up in court.

A Compendium of HMO Daddy's Blogs - £4.95
Downloadable version - £1.93

This collection of invaluable HMO advice and tips shared by Jim Haliburton covers tips for new investors into HMOs, costly mistakes to avoid, how to become a successful HMO investor, what makes a property investor different from a general investor, how to avoid LHA claims, unusual properties bought, how to evict unemployed tenants who refuse to pay and what is wrong with current housing standards.

Serviced Accommodation - £9.99
Downloadable version - £6.93

This book is an outline of the legalities involved in operating as Serviced Accommodation. I wrote this because when I first considered using some as my properties for Serviced Accommodation I could not find any information on the subject. I, therefore, researched the topic and have come up with this book.

To order any book or books please go to
WWW.HMODADDY.COM

Manuals

How to Become a Multimillionaire HMO Landlord - £597
Downloadable version - £497

Written by an experienced HMO Landlord with 140 properties and nearly 1000 rooms, originally written in 2005 and updated regularly, this manual stood the test of time and is the authorities guide to starting and setting up an HMO. The manual shows how HMO Daddy started and runs his HMO's and how you can do the same and covers the HMO market, acquiring the ideal property for an HMO, negotiating the right price, tenant selection, property management, property standards and general advice on property. The How to become a Multi-Millionaire Landlord manual will help novice or experienced single let landlords transform their property portfolios into profitable multi-million cash-flowing assets. A complete how to guide in one manual.

DIY Eviction - £125
Downloadable version- £99

Jim Haliburton (HMO Daddy) clearly explains using his experience of evicting over 300 tenants through the courts with 100% success and far more tenants without having to go court to evict. He shows by using the correct legal process it is possible to evict a problem tenant without the necessity of using a lawyer. This is the only DIY guide to evicting tenants and simply explains how to evict tenants and if they refuse to go how to use the legal process to successfully remove a tenant from your property cheaply, quickly, easily and legally. The guide tells you how to answer all the questions ever asked of Jim by judges in the eviction process and how to deal with things when the eviction goes wrong. It is recommended you buy this along with my book' HMOs and Compensation for Unlawful Eviction' see book section.

Operating Standards - £297
Downloadable version - £197

The operating Standards contain all the knowledge, the scripts, the tools and the systems to run your HMO Portfolio with clear step-by-step processes to manage any potential HMO issues.

The thought of starting or running an HMO portfolio can be very daunting as you do not know whose advice you can trust, how to get the legal right letting to tenants and inspecting properties.

The operating standards contain all the information you need to run your HMO and consistently build your income including customer care, letting criteria and arranging interviews, answering the telephone to prospective clients, showing premises, handing over premises, tenant rating, repairs and tenant requests, dealing with tenants, collection of rents and dealing with building works and renovations.

Implementing the Operating Standards has the potential to replace your salary in 12 months and contains plans and checklists to help you run your HMO efficiently and profitably or show staff how to do it.

Forms, Notices, Agreements and Manuals with memory stick - £225.00
Downloadable version - £125

The forms, Notices and Agreements manual covers all the relevant forms including application forms for tenants, tenancy pack, abandonment documentation, ASTs, Court forms and assorted notices for tenants including Section 8 Ground 8, 10 & 11 for landlords – 65 different forms, notices and agreements at the last count.

These forms, lists, notices and agreements are essential paperwork that all beginner or established landlords must have to run their property portfolios legally, efficiently and profitably.

How to Get Properties for Free (Almost) and Turn Them into Money Making Machines - £297.00
Downloadable version - £197

This is my latest manual and explains all the strategies I use to obtain properties for nothing or very little and how to make them cash flow giving a healthy profit after all costs in a question-and-answer style. There are over 80 questions and answers in the manual. Every question I have been asked in this area including the motivation needed have been answered. A gripping read!

**To order any books or manuals please
go to www.hmodaddy.com**

or

email jim@hmodaddy.com

Mentorships

HMO Academy

Work as an HMO Landlord – no charge

The HMO Academy 400-hour internship – come to us in Walsall for 400 hours over about 6 months – an average of a couple of days per week, or you can do it all in one go which should take you around 8 weeks you chose how you want to do it. Shadowing every department of our lettings company, you get a chance to assist with tenants' interviews, viewings, rent collection, maintenance and house conversion, and also spend time with the HMO Daddy training team acquiring new properties and planning their conversion.

By attending the HMO Daddy Academy, you will receive the extensive course manual and our operating standards for free which you are expected to read and understand. You will learn all the techniques you need to run your own portfolio and spend a lot of quality time with Jim Haliburton and the team....in return we ask you to work as requested in the various departments and bring whatever skills you have to the business. To apply we ask for your CV or summary of you and what you have done, some personal details and a deposit of £997. When you complete the 400 hours we return the £997 deposit. Free accommodation in my HMOs is available.

HMO Daddy offers limited bursaries for the above. If you are unable to afford the £997 deposit you can apply for a bursary to cover the deposit, your travel and subsistence.

One-to-One Consultations – phone, Skype call or face-to-face

Telephone, Skype call or face-to-face consultation. Are you too busy or not inclined to attend a course or just don't know where to start? Then you can have a one-to-one consultation with HMO Daddy or one of HMO Daddy's consultants.

With HMO Daddy	
30 minutes	£125
60 minutes	£250
Half day fee	£800
Full day fee	£1400

To book a one-to-one consultation please email jim@hmodaddy.com